Positive
Pasta
Publishing

Good Habits
Part 1

Written by
Ankit Kothari

Take a shower everyday

Positive Learning for Kids

Positive Pasta with Motivational Marinara™

Don't Be A Couch Potato!

Instead of sitting on the couch, Lion should play outside with her friends!

Reduce Your Phone Time!

How often are you on your phone?

Rather then using their phones, Ducklings should play outside!

Don't Color On
Yourself!

Do you like coloring on paper?

Rather than coloring on herself,
Elephant should color on paper!

Say Excuse Me!

Do you remember to always say excuse me?

Puppy says excuse me when he wants to get his friend's attention because it is polite!

Don't Run In The Street!

Camels should not run in the street because it is not safe!

Look Both Ways Before Crossing The Street!

Do you look both ways before you cross the street?

Sheep looks both ways before crossing the street to make sure there are no cars coming and it is safe!

Don't Eat Junk Food!

How often do you eat junk food?

Instead of eating junk food,
Squirrel Monkey should eat healthy,
so he can grow big and strong!

Read A Book!

What is your favorite book to read?

Mr. Guinea Pig reads every day because reading is fun!

Don't Bite Your Nails!

Do you bite your nails?

Monkey should not bite his nails, because there can be yucky germs in them!

Take A Shower
Everyday!

Do you shower
every day?

Dog always takes a shower
after playing outside to keep
himself clean!

Don't Fight With Friends!

Instead of fighting with each other, Tigers should try to play nice and have fun!

Say Sorry If You Make A Mistake!

Do you say sorry when you make a mistake?

12

Baby Seal always says sorry to Mommy Seal when he makes a mistake!

Don't Be Sad!

Sometimes Pug feels sad, but he should try to cheer up and be happy!

Be Happy!

14

Puppy tries to always be happy,
because life is better
when you are smiling!

Don't Stuff Your Face!

Do you think Chipmunk is being polite?

15

Chipmunk should not stuff her face because it is not polite!

Sit When You Are Eating!

Monkey knows to sit when he is eating to avoid choking!

Don't Talk Back To Your Parents!

Do you talk back to your parents?

17

Baby Goose should not talk back to Mommy Goose, because it is rude!

Always Buckle Your Seatbelt!

Do you always wear your seatbelt?

Dog should not unbuckle his seatbelt while the car is moving, because that is not safe!

Sharing is Caring!

Do you like to share with your friends and family?

Lemurs share their food with each other, because sharing is caring!

Always Say Thank you!

Do you say thank you when someone does you a favor?

20

Seal always says thank you, because he wants to thank people who are kind to him!

Go To Bed
Early!

How early do you go to bed?

21

Cat goes to bed early, so every morning she can have a fresh start to the day!

Wake Up Early!

Do you get up early in the morning?

Cows always wake up **early because** it starts their day off right!

Try To Avoid Getting Angry!

Have you ever been angry when you didn't get what you wanted?

23

Instead of being angry when Monkey does not get his way, he should try to remain calm!

Always Make Your Bed!

Do you make your bed every day?

Storks fix their nest every morning,
so it looks nice when vistors come over!

Cover Your Mouth When You Cough!

Do you always cover your mouth when you cough?

25

Monkey covers his mouth when he coughs, so he doesn't get his friends sick!

Keep Your Room Clean!

26

After making a mess, Bunnies always clean their room!

Acknowledgements

Hemanki Kothari
Nevaan Kothari
Riaan Kothari
Dilip Kothari
Hasumati Kothari
David Diaz

Edited By

Emily Kirsner

Facebook.com/PositivePosta
Instagram: @PositivePosta
Twitter: @Positive_Pasta

Made in the USA
Middletown, DE
21 November 2017